Civic Skills and Values

Fairness

By Dalton Rains

www.littlebluehousebooks.com

Copyright © 2024 by Little Blue House, Mendota Heights, MN 55120. All rights reserved. No part of this book may be reproduced or utilized in any form or by any means without written permission from the publisher.

Little Blue House is distributed by North Star Editions:
sales@northstareditions.com | 888-417-0195

Produced for Little Blue House by Red Line Editorial.

Photographs ©: Shutterstock Images, cover, 9, 11, 15 (top), 15 (bottom), 20–21, 24 (top right), 24 (bottom left), 24 (bottom right); iStockphoto, 4, 7, 12, 17, 18, 23, 24 (top left)

Library of Congress Control Number: 2022919842

ISBN
978-1-64619-815-3 (hardcover)
978-1-64619-844-3 (paperback)
978-1-64619-900-6 (ebook pdf)
978-1-64619-873-3 (hosted ebook)

Printed in the United States of America
Mankato, MN
082023

About the Author

Dalton Rains writes and edits nonfiction children's books. He lives in Minnesota.

Table of Contents

Fair and Square **5**

Struggles **13**

Think of Others **19**

Glossary **24**

Index **24**

Fair and Square

Fairness is about treating people right.

It means that everyone gets what they need.

Fairness matters when you play.
You do not leave anyone out.
You treat everyone the same.

Fairness can mean
taking turns.
You go on the swing.
Then you let your friend
have a turn.

Playing fair also means following the rules. That means everyone gets an equal chance.

Struggles

Sometimes fairness is easy.
You make sure both teams have the same number in tug-of-war.
The teams are fair.

Other times, it is hard. Maybe you did something harmful. You want to blame your sister, but you have to tell the truth.

School can be hard too. Your teacher might spend more time with a classmate than with you. That seems unfair, but she needs extra help.

Think of Others

Fairness means you think about others' feelings. You can share food so no one feels hungry.

You think about the other people at the fountain. They feel thirsty too. You drink quickly so they can have a turn.

Fairness happens in many ways. Treating people right helps everyone have fun.

Glossary

classmate

swing

fountain

tug-of-war

Index

B
blame, 14

D
drink, 20

R
rules, 10

S
school, 16